Voices Draped in Black

Voices Draped in Black

Poems by

Ifi Amadiume

Africa World Press, Inc.

P.O. Box 1892   P.O. Box 48
Trenton, NJ 08607   Asmara, ERITREA

Africa World Press, Inc.

P.O. Box 1892
Trenton, NJ 08607

P.O. Box 48
Asmara, ERITREA

Cover art: Kemdi Amadiume
Cover design: Ashraful Haque
Book design: Aliya Books

Library of Congress Cataloging-in-Publication Data

Amadiume, Ifi, 1947-
 Voices draped in black : poems / by Ifi Amadiume.
    p. cm.
  ISBN 1-59221-592-0 -- ISBN 1-59221-593-9 (pbk.)
 1. Political activists--Poetry. I. Title.

PR9387.9.A4855V65 2007
821'.914--dc22

                              2007027261

Contents

Dedication

This new collection contains poems written intermittently from the 1980s to the present, celebrating activism and activists, known and unknown, women and men, and the spirit of struggle. Some were assassinated, while some are still alive and some have since passed away. They all have left behind a strong legacy of their commitment and courage.

Women Activists

In Praise of an African Woman Activist

In your shining eyes,
the inextinguishable
political fire of love
burns strong,
      Althea,
      sista,
      lady,
      rebel woman,
         my friend!

In your sing-song
rolling accent
from Afrikan Trinidad,
Afrika in the Caribbean,
the political fire of Truth
sounds so strong,
      Althea,
      sista,
      lady,
      rebel woman,
         my friend!

Inside a special place
in my authentic
Afrikan heart
is your safe place of love,
      Althea,
      sista,
      lady,
      rebel woman,
         my friend!

With all the political
      burnings,
      meetings,
      speeches,

                    sobs,
                    tears,
          and anger,

We can only do our best,
our damned best
and leave the rest
to our open-eyed children,
our politicized babes,
fruits of an uneasy choice,
                    Nandi!
                    Kemdi!
                    Amadi!
          daat little Ifi!
beautiful children of
Our Mother, Mami Mbuya Nehanda!
small children of
Our Mother, Nneanyi Idemili!
strong children of
Our Mother, Maroon Nanny!
children of the Mothers
and the Mothers before!

You have done your very best,
                    Althea,
                    sista,
                    lady,
                    rebel woman,
                          my friend!

(London, August 1991)

Fatima Ibrahim

(Speaking at Africa Centre, London, 10/12/92)

Dark shadows around her brightly burning eyes,
fingers pointing, stressing serious points,
Now she spreads her ever moving hands,
Next she makes her ever intriguing signs,
as she shares knowledge oozing from her ignited mind.

Now it is a flash of her even white teeth,
Now a trace of light sparkles in her narrowed eyes,
Next a full view of her beautiful face
above a silky blue veil,
softly wrapped under her rounded cheeks,
as she reaches out to this excited crowd with grace.

It is Fatima Ibrahim
gaining political points!
One time imprisoned!
One time widowed!
One time outlawed!

This Fatima woman!
mother, feminist, unionist!
This political activist,
This rebel woman
firing my soul with
her wonderful women's movement!

For Angela Davis

(MIT Boston, Jan 15, 1994)

Every move, Angela, every move!
No more, no less will satisfy
these hungry eyes of mine
set right at the centre,
where I hurried to gain a seat,
to listen, to hear,
to let your words enter,
to see you!

I have sung the sisters,
I have sung their praises!
I have sung the mothers,
I have celebrated the lovers!

With this one, Angela,
there can be no praising,
no songs of celebration,
for as you say,
"these are dangerous times!"

So wear this necklace,
with its African drum,
beating its tum tum,
soundings of life,
soundings of things long gone,
soundings of things still to come,
soundings, soundings, soundings,
sounds and soundings,
next to your heart, Angela,
and we say,
A lutta! a lutta!
as the struggle continues!

Edidi—Oo

(Edith Ihekweazu, who died in a car accident - Sept 1991)

A silu n'Edidi nwulu?
Onwu-oo!
Alu-oo!

A silu n'o Edidi,
nwanyi Ihekweazu
k'asidenti gbulu?
onwu-oo!
alu-oo!

Awu-uu ife melu!
Awu-uu alu eme-ee!
Alu eme anyi-oo!
Alu emekwana anyi-oo!

Onwu agbanyi ose n'anya-oo!
Onwu ebulu nwanne anyi-oo!
Onwu egbue nwanyi ibe anyi-oo!

Haa! Edidi!
O k'idi?
Ha! Ha! Ha!

Edidi!
O k'anyi si jezi?
    gini mezi?
  gini k'emel'i?
gini k'imel' anyi?
kezi if'anyi mel'i?
kezi if'anyi g'eme?
Haa! Ha! Ha! Ha!

Gwam onye oma!
Gwam nwanyi oma!
Gwam nwanyi ezigbo omume!
Kwue k'ife silu me!

Kunie kwue –O!
Kunie kwue okwu –O!
Kunie, kunie –O!
Bikozinu, biko –O!

Oji ugo!
Onwa n'etil'Igbo!
Oji ugo!
Ana mmuo-oo!

Oji ugo!
onwa n'ekwul'Igbo!
Oji ugo!
Ana mmuo-oo!

Oji ugo!
Nwanyi Igbo!
Oji ugo!
O naa ana mmuo!

Oji ugo!
Nne um'Igbo!
Oji ugo!
O nakwana ana mmuo!

Edidi anakwana!
Edidi anakwana!
Oyoyo anakwana!
Onwa na nganga ya!
        Onakwana!
        Ona-aaaa!
        Onakwana!

Uwanka ife-eee!
        ife-eee!
Uwanka ofia-aa!
        ofia-aa!
Uwanka igwe-ee!
        igwe-ee!

Olujue-eeeeeee!
Olujugo-oooooo!

Edidi-ooooooo!
Edidi-ooooooo!

(London, Sept. 1991)

Oh Edith!

(My Translation)

Edith is dead?
Oh death, death!
Oh woe, woe!

Edith,
wife of Ihekweazu,
killed in accident?
Oh death, death!
Woe to death!
Woe to death!

Something horrible has come to pass!
Something terrible has happened to us!

Death has spat hot pepper
into our eyes!
Death has stolen our sister!
Death has killed our sister woman!

Haa! Edith!
So this is how you are!
Haa! ha! ha!

Edith!
So this is it?
What happened?
What was done to you?
What have you done to us?
What wrong have we done you?
What shall we do?
Haa! ha! ha!
Tell me beautiful one!
Tell me beautiful woman!
Tell me kind woman!
Say what happened, please!

Rise and speak, please!
Rise and talk, please!
Rise, rise, please!
Please! please!

Precious white kolanut!
Full moon that shines for Ndigbo!
Precious white kolanut!
She has gone to land of the dead!

Precious white kolanut!
Voice that speaks for Ndigbo!
Precious white kolanut!
She has gone to land of the dead!

Precious white kolanut!
Beautiful wife of Ndigbo!
Precious white kolanut!
She has gone to land of the dead!

Precious white kolanut!
Beloved mother of Ndigbo!
Precious white kolanut!
She has gone to land of the dead!

Edith has gone!
Edith has gone!
Beautiful one has gone!
Like the moon and all her wiles!
She has gone!
She has gone!

This world is something else!
        something else!
This world is like the forest!
        like the forest!
This world is like the clouds!
        like the clouds!
            Oh! dark clouds!

Oh! dark clouds!

Oh Edith!
Oh Edith!

Men Activists

Viva Babu

(To The Memory of My Friend Babu, September 22, 1924 -
August 5, 1996, laid in state Wed. August 7 at the Africa
Centre, London.)

I had not come back to London
to bury you my dear friend and teacher!
how could that be when the stories
are yet to end!
Oh how my heart aches with pain,
sorrow, even confusion.
You never once left my thoughts;
how could that be when you had
lit up the fire of my imagination
with your teachings, your stories
about doing somethings
about revolution inside the bush!
the workers and the peasants
had your support!
Zanzibar saw your hand!
Che knew you!
Malcolm X heard you!
Nkrumah too!
Many many more!

You who pursued revolution into exile!
60s discourse is incomplete without your voice!
The comrades have called you
"African giant",
"passionate pan-Africanist",
"communist thinker",
"reformist socialist",
"a great scholar",
"a smiling rebel",
above all, " a free spirit"!

Ifi Amadiume

To know you was to learn truth in simplicity;
no vainglorious deceiving glamour.
You asked only for our comradery tears for farewell;
nothing more, nothing pompous,
just the fighter's simple shroud.
Remember how you once told me
you would like to visit Kaolack,
then I knew of a private longing
sacrificed for the bigger struggle;
now even the mountain came to Muhammad,
for I could scent the aromas of Kaolack,
see the crescent moon and a shining star,
as you lay shrouded in Africa Center,
words from the Qur'an written on black silk,
the air was filled with sadness,
I saw young men groan in pain,
sobbing as their shoulders shook like earth quake!
Little did we expect this sudden passing,
Oh Abdulrahamanu Muhammadu Babu!

To know you was to know victory was possible,
your steady faith and courage,
the proven heroism of your life,
radicalizing the youth,
advancing revolutionary consciousness,
always a worldwide ideal of struggle
for a socialist Africa!

Nothing will be lost,
that is the promise of our love,
as we begin to pick your words,
reclaim your thoughts,
trace your actions,
follow every move,
every step an upward surge!!
oh precious friend,
teacher, father, comrade,
onward to victory!

Only the authentic salute suits you:
After Lenin,
Mao,
Lumumba,
Babu!
Viva!
Ever onward to victory!

The Claudian Key Words

(For Claude Ake, February 18, 1939 - November 7, 1996,
who died in a plane crash)

Claude,
the first time that
I knew of you,
you were a Zed Press first;
red Claude talking revolution.

Decades on,
you were still causing concern.
That was last year,
when you made me
your keynote speaker,
and the talk was for
revolutionary consolidation,
this time for sister comrades.
Hear Claude,
"We must begin to reach for
a paradigm that integrates
women's rights and health rights
in the context of culture and development".

The Claudian key words
remained unchanged,
as you hammered on:
policy, advocacy,
face tightened with
determination, passion,
you emphasized
academic activism,
mechanism,
and how to keep
our consortium of ideas
inside and outside,
nationally and internationally.

How the sisters have cried you
with hot hot tears in our eyes!
Oh how the heart burns,
choking with pain
in this unwarranted
loss of our brother, so brave.

I took my crying for Claude
and went searching the clouds.
I took my weeping for our son
and went gazing into the sea.

"What good is this searching
everyday in the wrong places,
eyes fixed on the clouds,
looking faraway for Claude",
said the water goddess.
"Think what your brother left you.
Don't you have the mirror with words?
Go search your brave comrade
in the mirror of fame,
where there is no forgetting."

There it was;
now how can we forget,
when even the internet,
Alta Vista Web Page,
to be precise,
gives me in batches of twenties, no less than
twenty five thousand and forty-seven
matches containing Claude Ake!
Director, CASS,
your revolutionary spirit
will never die,
as the struggle continues!!

(Dartmouth College
Nov. 19, 1996.)

Ifi Amadiume   19

Rage for Chris Hani
(Assassinated October 4, 1993)

My father Mandela
is talking for them,
for them, for them,
not for me, not for me!
He is not talking for me!

My father Mandela
is talking for them,
for them, for them, for them,
not for Hani, not for Hani!
He is not talking for Hani!

Even with Chris killed,
my father Nelson Mandela
still talks for them,
for them, for them, for them!
He is not talking for Chris!

Even with us bleeding,
our father Nelson Mandela
still talks as a messenger
for them. for them, for them!
He is not talking for us!

Even in our burning rage,
our father Nelson Mandela
still talks for them!
Not for our dead, our dead!
He is not talking for our dead!

Even as we rage, burn, die,
our father Nelson Mandela
still talks with them!
They talk, talk, talk,
as we burn, burn, burn!

As we rage for Chris Hani,
As we burn for Chris Hani,
As we die with Chris Hani,
As we struggle for our Azania!

Oh Africa! Our Africa!
It is bullets, bullets, bullets!
Everywhere is bullets, bullets!
Everywhere we are dying, dying!
Just dying, dying, dying!

(April 15, 1993)

Pa Mandela and the Slippery Steps

"O pardon me thou bleeding
piece of earth
    That I am meek and gentle
with these butchers."

(Nelson Mandela quoting William Shakespeare in his address to the British Parliament in Westminster Hall, July 11, 1996)

Betty Boothroyd wearing a man's wig,
woman speaker of a whiteman's House
never mind they lie it is the Commons;
This Betty woman helped Pa Mandela
to go down the velvety carpet,
too red for the African bull,
fighting like hell
to keep angry memories low key.

Did this same House not once
ask for his African head?
Oh the hypocrisy of this Britain again!

Strong with prison-learnt patient tactics,
Pa Mandela made it down the slippery steps!

Where little kids saw fun in a jolly old man,
and the Black community sang about
their waiting, their love for their hero man,
shameless racists read irenic,
by which they say they mean placid,
since they had the old man
talking investment, inviting
the greedy butchers, let's say
calling the hyena to come guard meat!
Oh the hypocrisy of this Britain again!

Those that are used to raging
were quick to read his lips.
We ourselves heard the low
rumbling of the African lion.
For did he not recall
the unforgettable humiliation;
the shaming eighty years ago
of the common African man?
Did Mandela not voice
their eloquence, their passion,
their human rights,
their right to liberty,
as he recalled that
unforgettable insulting of Africa,
of the common African
citizen of the soil
eighty years ago!

For placid, we read admonition
of the same racism of enslavement!
the same racism of colonialism!
the same racism of the Grand Disaster of apartheid!
the same racism of capitalist imperialism!

For Godsake, in saying no to apartheid,
who simply performed?
who truly raged?
outside South Africa House.

Yes, Pa Mandela said,
racism is in truth a sickness!
Pa Mandela asked,
why did we allow these crimes
against humanity to happen?
Never again shall "our voices be stilled
if we see that another elsewhere in the world
is victim to racial tyranny".

For Godsake, in saying no to apartheid,
who simply performed?
who truly raged?
outside South Africa House.

Pa Mandela's democracy is
non-racist, non-sexist!
and all those big bad white men
are still ruling the world!
Oh the hypocrisy of this Britain again!

For Godsake, in saying no to apartheid,
who simply performed?
who truly raged?
outside South Africa House.

Pa talked about the new Jeremiahs of blame
we have to lay another vigil of rage against.
Oh the hypocrisy of this Britain again!
I say that raging must include
going to our Winnie in friendship,
finding our Winnie in friendship,
forgiving our Winnie in friendship,
for the struggle continues.
Cannibalistic capitalism
isn't our destiny!

For Godsake, we said no to apartheid,
who these days is the captain of capital?
Who is eating who?

(London, July 12, 1996)

Pa Mandela, We Thank You, We Love You!

At 87, I imagine you to say,
my mouth has talked the talk,
my legs have walked the walk,
these hands have crushed hard rock,
my eyes blinded by poisonous dust,
my name erased,
branded prisoner number 46664!

All in all I have kept promises made
to my people,
to my Africa,
to humanity,
to the world.

My generation carried the struggle
like a very special pregnancy
that is conceived in later years,
nurtured, protected from danger
so I have carried Azania and Africa.

Struggle is tough,
love even tougher,
it would seem!

You do not rock the boat,
the dream of Azania
was our baby,
a free Africa
was our call
and we gave all!

Yes, that is one thing
I know for sure;
you have loved our people
Africa, humanity, the world

Ifi Amadiume

Pa Mandela, thank you!
and we love you!
This is the least we can say to you at 87!

(Dartmouth College, July 26, 2005)

The Soyinka Poems

For Dele Giwa

(The Giant Elephant of News, bombed to smithereens
October 19, 1986, following intensive harassment and
hounding by the Nigerian security agents.)

In this war against the people,
where crime is seen to win,
where inflation degradation,
unemployment depression,
retrenchment desperation,
have turned our people
uninformed helpers in crime!

In this land of ours,
where the spoils of power
loom large in giant structures
mocking the homeless masses,
where women wail at night,
where with broken bottles,
smoking pistols,
evil reigns in this our violated land,
as armed men,
men of power,
war against the people!

Where they shoot students!
Where virgin school girls bleed!
in their violated sacred thighs!

Where they kill Trade Unionists!
Where these parasitical thieves
in the towers of power
eat-off market women's backs!

Where they blow to pieces
angered youths demanding Truth!
Where they silence
outraged radicals speaking Truth!

In this mind-boggling land of ours,
where evil seems endemic,
where hunger for the masses is an unending epidemic,
with corruption strong in the corridors of power!
Words of truth never ran dry
from the powerful pen
in the steady hand
of the ever-wakeful Newswatcher,
the man they called Dele Giwa!

That hand is stilled today!
his pen unfinished today!
Hero of the pen
blown out of history
into legend in one day!

When the pen is struck
and the tears of sorrow
begin to flow,
then will the power of words
reign supreme,
crying the dead!

Was ever a man
better mourned than
Dele, the son of Giwa?
Dele, the giant elephant of news!
Chief Newswatcher!

"Colourful like the rainbow"!
"beating in beauty
the royal pageant"!
"specially spectacular'!
"surpassing a kaleidoscope"!
"a smashing lagoon
of one-thousand regattas,
as if reflecting
a thousand and one
sparkling celestial stars"!

Ah! Sina Odugbemi!
May the gods cool
your heaving heart!
May the gods beat
their comforting hands
on your stout chest
ready to burst!
Vanguard mourner
in a wounded nation,
crying the dead,
"Dele came at you
with a pen
dripping a viper's venom",
you wrote!

Dele, the man
who claimed front page
in life and in death!
and you said,
"he was a white tiger,
ruler of the open field";

like the torrential downpour
of the mighty rains of June,
he will thunder for basic truth!
In lucidity strong too!

I do not myself recall
this kind of crying
any other time in my life,
maybe when mama died;
she too left young!

I find myself, today,
an endless well of tears,
as they keep repeating
news of the murder
of Dele Giwa,
a man I have never seen!

Ifi Amadiume

a man I might never have met!
Yet, have met indeed;
his fearlessness,
his forthrightness,
that unrelentless
pursuit of truth!

Dele, the ensurer of justice!
Dele, the best mixer
of brain-fire and pen!
Giant who bestrides
the news world!

The struggle continues,
as we fill the barrels of our pens!
as we fight these bloody beasts!
as we fight their agents of regression!

The struggle continues, for
On our side the Truth!
On our side the spirit!
On our side the Truth that never lies!
On our side the spirit that never dies!

Ever daring Dele!
Soon the poet-piper,
Our own Wole Soyinka,
Poet Laureate,
from this same our land
will sing for you!
Ogun will say your name!
For the spirit never dies!

(Enugu, Nigeria, October 1986)

Reply to Wole Soyinka

(on the uniformed men and the state of the nation, THE
PUNCH, November 2 and 5, 1992)

Wole,
I have read you.
I used to read you.
Then, my girlish heart
invented an unseen lover —
a bushy-haired, sandal-shoed,
well known rebel!

Today, again,
in our collective pain
I read you,
and my woman's heart
warms up to the challenges
of the struggle at hand!

Last time I read you,
they had killed Dele Giwa.
Again, in our collective despair,
we had cried out loud.
We had mourned a brave youth!
His bomb-blasted head
smashed to pieces!
We mourned an audacious
Newswatcher silenced forever!

In his brutal death,
we had also seen
the ugly face of the butcher
telling of the season
of terror in store.
Then Wole,
how you wrote!
How you spoke!
How I read you!

Ifi Amadiume   33

Then, I too wrote!
     I spoke!
     I wept!
     I left!

But the greedy beast refuses to leave!
The brazen thieves stay on,
as madam swells remorselessly imperious,
spitting abusive contempt
from her blood-red lips,

"Who said we are leaving?
"Who ever spoke of leaving?

"All your best,
"do they not serve me?

"Even your richest
"owe their riches to me!

"I that can make
"and unmake!

"Who the hell
"talked of ever leaving?

But, Wole,
you ought to know,
Madam also said,
"even that one-time
bushy-haired,
sandal-shoed rebel,
you all used to know,
he too wines and dines with me!
Give him media time what can he say!"

Reply by Wole Soyinka
(for Ifi Amadiume)

"Oh my dear Ifi
How strange it should be you
That gave a lie poetic wings
And launched it free
To breed and molt.
High ladies of the realm
Are also mortal,
Prone to fantasies,
And the odd exalted fib."

Signed by Wole Soyinka
(January 19, 1993)

For Wole Soyinka

That Ogun should groan, pained?
Not pound his iron fist, roaring
like thunder?
He knows 'tis best
the wounding words said
in the fairness of love,
in the anger of struggle,
than the danger of silence,
born of cold indifference.

(February 1, 1993)

In Solidarity
(For Wole Soyinka - March 22, 1995)

To abandon or ignore?
To regret or forget?
To criticize or solidarity?
So the dialogue with self,
a new talking to oneself,
atomized, demoralized,
isolated in struggle!

A new talking form
to unburden, unload,
as I rock myself
to quietness and vigil.

At 33,000 feet, floating
after another returning,
for I have even returned
again!
Yes!
I know
I said
I cried
I left!

What choice when duty calls?
That is one way of returning.
There is the other returning in mind.
The thought of one dearly loved.
No moment passed without remembering in silent pain
harsh words that were said.

How the sight of you these days
send onion stings and then it rains!
The bushiness of hair.
The grayness of unkept beard.
Your thinness, your sadness, your restlessness,

above all your pain!
These sights of you reawaken
those old concerns of one who vowed to love,
to continue to love in solidarity to the end.

Together dear friend,
we are walking the miles.
Together dear friend,
we struggle!
What then but to keep returning!
I share your pain, our pain, our struggle,
until the beast is no more!

Struggle

Biafra

When the nearby empty church bell strikes three,
the tattered boots sound their terrible presence;
it is at three that they always pass by.

As I hide heart pounding with fear
under the coconut tree,
in the far distant sky,
I still can see the sun shinning brightly,
cold shivers run down my spine,
as my heart pounds like a punctured exhaust pipe
at the strike of three.

I wonder how many will return,
I wonder what tomorrow will bring,
who will pass away,
who will pass this way again.

They are Biafran boys,
children of the rising sun,
living minute by minute in dangerous daring,
young kids with no ammo as they say,
boys with blazing eyes,
mouths spitting angry songs,
sweats pouring down their faces,
determined, courageous,
they burn like fire,
they sing sad songs in unison,
like bellows they set the air aflame.

I wonder how many will return,
I wonder what tomorrow will bring,
who will pass away,
who will pass this way again.

Hiding under the coconut tree,
I have seen the brutality of war,

a kindred, babies, children and more
torn to shreds in futile death.
Hiding under the coconut tree,
I have heard the sounds of war,
more frightening than tropical thunder,
descending from distant hills,
pouring down from an electrified sky.

Hiding under the coconut tree,
I have felt my very tongue freeze,
that is when nothing moves,
not even the sound of breeze,
then bitter pangs of pain
do their churning, turning, twisting,
in stomach weakened
with the nervousness of emptiness,
with fear of distant battles,
the unnerving sound of shelling,
bombs pounding in heavy bombardment,
bullets raining down explosives,
precious lives cheapened in convulsive hate!

We all learned to hide and wait,
even little children learned to live in fear!

Hiding under the coconut tree,
I have seen many pass by,
I have seen the brutality of war,
when very few return,
when children cry with fear,
disarmed with fear,
weakened by starvation,
all for Biafra,
a bride killed at the alter!

Elegy for Christopher Okigbo—Through Labyrinths*

(Okigbo 1932–1967, acclaimed twentieth century poet who died in August 1967 in the war front fighting for Biafra in the Nigeria-Biafra war, 1967–1970.)

1.

These ten years
of tender tears
lost in your mind,
a follower! O Okigbo!

I have followed;
I, the fluffy feathered chick,
you, the full fledged hen!
Mother, I have followed!

I have followed you, Mother,
full heartedly,
even to Heavensgate,
to the sacred passage,
behind the holy **ogilisi*** tree.

I have followed, Mother,
to the point where Okigbo,
long-gone child of my mother,
in fragile nakedness stood,
facing the river between,
lost in the spell of **IDOTO***,
child of the great woman,
our water Goddess, **IDEMILI***!

I have followed, Mother,
to the point
where I heard Okigbo wailing
at Heavensgate!
to the point

where I heard **nwannem*** sobbing
at Heavensgate!
to the point
where I heard the secret oracle!
The telling of the doom to come!

*Christopher Okigbo, *Labyrinths: With Path of Thunder,*
London: Heinemann, 1971.
*ogilisi - oilbean tree.
*Idoto – a river and a goddess.
*Idemili – a river and a goddess
*nwannem – my sibling.

2.

Oh Okigbo!
I have followed
in your footsteps!
A wandering seeker!
You have shown me
mere glimpses
of your promises
of short rays of violets
to ease the gloom!
The promised light
remains
hazily remembered
dreams at night!

Oh Okigbo!
how I have followed
in your footsteps!
A solitude wretch,
tailing
a young sunbird,
waiting
a mum long dead,
come rain, come sunshine,

single-minded,
at the sacred passage!

Oh Okigbo!
these ten years,
in longing,
I have followed Mother
to the point
where you stood supreme,
heavenly haloed,
at Heavensgate!

3.

I have followed,
one long-faced child,
in the solid column of ants!
and Anna?
Okigbo's piano player-mother,
Queen bee in black,
mourners in
a festivity without joy!

I have followed,
one sullen-faced child,
in the singing band of girls,
sisters of the departed dead,
in ringed circles,
around freshly dug,
dark-red earth,
for a festivity without joy!

I have followed,
one last time,
a wide-eyed maiden,
unwilling witness
to my brother's sacred passage!
a broken-hearted girl,
at Heavensgate!

4.

Upon the riverbed,
oh brother of my mother-bred,
we stood,
hand in hand,
in somber mood,
heart to heart,
twin-witnesses
to your secret,
planted in whitened sand!

Upon the river tomb,
oh child of a shared womb,
we looked,
holding fevered hands,
florescent ghostlike,
on the bleached sand,
and I,
a witness
to your secret
of the water maid!

Upon the riverbed,
oh departed brother,
stands your sister,
wretched,
abandoned,
counting secrets in sea-sand!
As you would say,
"*sprinkled with memories*"!
I stand,
re-memorying faces of old!

Upon the riverbed,
I wait,
long past the stars are dead!
I wait,
breathless,

to clutch at
the fleeting
moment of secrets
of the water maid remembered!

5.

So I have to the riverbed.
So I have,
to where **IDEMILI** becomes **IDOTO**,
there to remember you.

And on the green riverbed,
naked, body and soul,
rain-washed in the full moon,
there to learn from you.

So I have in ecstatic abandon.
So I have
lain waiting,
child of daughter **EDO***,
reigning Queen of **OJOTO***.

Here one more daughter,
egg and chick in hand,
I stand,
humble at the secret passage,
before the source
of the sacred spring!
Here I stand,
the silent sister
in lament I sing!

*Edo, a goddess and daughter of the goddess Idemili.
*Ojoto, Ojoto-Nnewi is Okigbo's home village.

6.

Ever following in your footsteps,
with you as chief drummer,

---

the chant of battle swelling,
even deep in the forbidden valley,
rumbling well past the impatient sunset!

Even upon the deserted hills,
your voice had learnt well
to bellow its NO in thunder!
Roaring deep in the forbidden valley!
raging well past the impatient sunset!

Ever following in your footsteps,
I joined the wailing for the Great River!
I witnessed my brother, chief drummer
of the masked dancers in the forefront!
From the distant hills, cannons blasted,
as I joined the lament of the drums!

7.

Dressed in ghost white,
crossed in bright red,
summoned in war service,
at the Red-Cross site,
I still heard your thunder,
even as my trembling hands
washed bleeding tendons,
tattered flesh and broken bodies
of brave young men!

I could hear your thunder!
Yes! Your thunderous No!
Okigbo, town-crier!
You sounded prophesy
in your iron bell,
defying their death sentence!
Yes! daring that deadly ambush
in the corridors of power!

And **COME THUNDER**:
"The death sentence lies in ambush along the corridors of
power;
And a great fearful thing already tugs at the cables of the open
air,
A nebula immense and immeasurable, a night of deep waters -
An iron dream unnamed and unprintable, a path of stone ...
The arrows of God tremble at the gates of light,
The drums of curfew pander to a dance of death. . ."

Dressed in ghost white,
crossed in bright red,
summoned in war service,
at the Red-Cross post.
I stood and saw you go
with Tom and Co!
Even as my trembling hands
waved goodbye,
I could still hear your thunder!

8.

I joined the wailing
for the field of crops.
I joined the wailing
for the field of men.
I joined the wailing
for the water Goddess.

From flesh into phantom,
at the sacred passage,
I was sole witness
to my brother's homecoming.

In a night without light,
his head like smashed fruit,
scattered between my feet,
his limbs like dry wood,
split in countless pieces,

Ifi Amadiume   49

his precious pool of blood,
spilling from my valleyed legs!

From flesh into phantom,
at the sacred passage,
I was sole witness
to my brother's homecoming!

In a night without drums,
in a night without silver bells,
in a night of anguish and solitude,
in a night of lusterless eyes,
the night that made me a pilgrim!

9.

From flesh into phantom,
at the sacred passage,
I was sole witness
to my brother's homecoming!

In nights of anguish and solitude,
upon the riverbank
"sprinkled with memories",
I can still hear Okigbo calling
from **DISTANCES**:
"Come into my cavern,
Shake the mildew from your hair;
Let your ear listen:
My mouth calls from a cavern...

Lo, it is the same blood that flows. . .

~~*For it is the same blood,*~~
through the same orifices,
the same branches
trembling intertwined,
and the same faces
in the interspaces.

And it is the same breath, liquid, without acolyte,
like invisible mushrooms on stone surfaces.

And at this chaste instant of delineated anguish,
the same voice, importunate, aglow with the goddess - . . .

and in the orangery of immense corridors,
I wash my feet in your pure head, O maid,

and walk along your feverish, solitary shores . . ."

10.

In nights of anguish and solitude,
upon the riverbank,
"sprinkled with memories",
I hear my brother

in **ELEGY OF THE WIND**:
"The ashes resolve their moments
Of twin-drops of dew on a leaf:
And like motion into stillness in my divine rejoicing -
The man embodies the child
The child embodies the man; the man remembers
The song of the innocent,
Of the uncircumcised at the sight of the flaming razor -

The chief priest of the sanctuary has uttered
           the enchanted words;
The bleeding phallus,
Dripping fresh from the carnage cries out for
           the medicinal leaf...

The child in me trembles before the high shelf
           on the wall,
The man in me shrinks before the narrow neck of
           a calabash;

And the chant, already all wings, follows
In its ivory circuit behind the thunder clouds,
The slick route of the feathered serpent..."

Ifi Amadiume   51

In nights of anguish and solitude,
upon the riverbank,
"*sprinkled with memories*",
I hear Okigbo
in **ELEGY FOR A SLIT-DRUM**:
"*condolences... from our swollen lips laden with*
condolences:
The mythmaker accompanies us
The rattles are here with us

condolences from our split-tongue of the slit drum condolences

one tongue full of fire
one tongue full of stone -

condolences from the twin-lips of our drum parted in
condolences..."

From flesh into phantom,
at the sacred passage,
I was sole witness
to my brother's homecoming!

(London, February 1993)

Favored Son of the Goddess

(In praise of Chinua Achebe on the publication of his
woman-centered novel, *Anthills of the Savannah,* 1988)

Said the Goddess Idemili,
Great old woman;
Woman with ivory wristlets;
Woman with ivory anklets;
Woman whose mercy
shields all her children;
Woman whose canoe of bounty
carries all safely home;
A towering pillar of grace;
Woman whose river
at all seasons is never empty;
Woman of the ivory-wristlets;
Woman whose messenger python
reveals all in dream;
Said she to her favorite son Chinua,

"Oh favorite of children,
your journey has been a long one.
You are weary and long to sit down;
you thirst for white wine of the great palm.
Your sisters, children of the womb-mother,
their hairs newly plaited,
bodies beautifully painted,
wait in readiness,
with rounded reddish pots,
cleverly balanced
on their padded heads.

But watch out for the hidden porcupine,
signaling their minds,
oh my favored one;
your sisters of the womb demand more!
Insatiable daughters of mine,

---

drinking pride, joy, anger, mischief,
all from one big cup!
Watch out for their prickly spikes
hidden in your seat!
They wait with song and dance,
one by one,
you will pick out the spikes,
now revealed before your very eyes.
There are more spikes to remove,
they are spikes of the people
with wickedness in their eyes,
wickedness in their tongue,
wickedness against us women,
wickedness against us sisters,
wickedness against us mothers
who bring all into this world,
who nourish all to manhood.

Oh favored child of mine,
your supplications reached me;
your work has come home.
Through your sisters,
I gave the holy sign;
now you wear white feathers
in your red cap!
Your tongue has been washed
to speak truth!
Wise man of my people,
you are home among our people,
your sisters will drop
their tears like a string of precious pearls
on your hands that command pen and ink
to do the great work of the people,
as you continue to pick out the spikes,
one by one,
so that we can all sit down
for a rest well deserved.

So have I spoken,
my word is law,
there is no man above me,
No! No!
No man reigns above my naked head."

So spoke the Goddess Idemili
to her favored son Chinua,
mixing love and law
in the manner of divine deities.

In praise of heroic deeds,
the Eagle feather,
like a handshake
of great thanks
graces the cap of our heroes.

When the elder speaks out,
the expectant youth listen
as if to say,
nowadays, we journey together,
but for the times before now,
please, please release
the wise words of wisdom
that you have that came before now.

So too, an expectant child
keeps on gazing outside
for a mother's return
from the market
with something!

Just as it is said that
you don't kindle fire
to observe daylight,
we also say
that the mouth does not
visit a fellow mouth
and return empty handed,

for however long the neck,
the head sits upon it.
But, like a bird
that flies into the bush is not lost,
so too a palm fruit that falls into a pot of oil
says it is home!

Boipatong Massacre 1992

Boipatong 1992!
tears were burning hot,
like flames under a cooking pot!

Boipatong, Boipatong,
tears were pouring
down the sides of faces mourning!

Counting in Boipatong?
Ai e e e! so many dead!
No mercy for anybody!
More tears were
pouring down the faces
counting Africans dead!

LA April 1992!
Nigeria May 1992!
Boipatong June 1992!
Ai e e e!
Ai! ai! ai!
Our dead?
Like scattered bullets on the ground!
Just like sand sand!

Africans died
of bullets, bullets,
like sand sand!
Africans are dying
just like sand sand!
from wicked men behind guns,
trigger happy, ready to pull it!

Bullets were everywhere!
Again bullets are flying through the air!
bullets, bullets, bullets!

Everywhere is cruelty and death,
from bullets, bullets, bullets!

Boipatong Raw Violence

Chopped up bodies
of African babies
in tattered clothes,
blood soaked bodies
of their murdered mums,
wrapped like garbage
in dirty blankets,
newspapers of old forgotten news.

How you mock
these lying intellectuals,
sleek in clothes,
drunk on rhetoric,
pompous speechifying cowards,
packaged in expensive white men's suits!

How you mock
these stupid
phrase-mongering fools!
these sickening
empty political rallies!
these silly men
in sleezy jet-black limousines,
politicians in shinny
long Cadillac cars,
snaking hurriedly through
rough neglected village roads,
as our people swarm old vans
like big black flies!

How these shameless men
make mockery of our dead!
clerics resplendent
in crimson cassocks!
How they read

well rehearsed speeches,
as they even shed
their crocodile tears!

The burials continue.
the killings continue.
the lamenting cries
of the masses continue!

Oh Boipatong, Boipatong,
it is raw violence,
raw raw violence,
raw violence,
raw violence,
as Africans die like flies!
as we die like flies!
as Africans die, die, die!
as we die, die, die!
we are dying like flies!

Boipatong Talks

My father Mandela
is holding the microphone.
My father Mandela
is looking at me,
but my father Mandela
is not talking to me.

He is talking to them.
He is looking at them.
He is saying to them,
". . . I can no longer
justify to my people. . ."

My father Mandela
is not talking to me!
it is not to me!
it is not to me!
   not to us!
   no not to us!

Boipatong, Boipatong,
as we burn, burn, burn,
they talk, talk, talk!
As we die die, die,
they walk, walk, walk!
they talk, talk, talk!
to them to them to them!
not to us!
no, not to us!

(July 1992)

The Slave House of Gorée

I have seen the Slave House of Gorée!
That horrible place where the putrid smell
of death, decay and misery lingers on,
as if it were the old days of slavery!

Gorée!
Who owns Gorée?
Who will own up to Gorée?
A symbol of Africa's enslavement!
T'is easy for them to forget
the shame of enslavement!

Between Dakar and the Island of Gorée,
t'is less than two miles,
no more than a 20-minute boat-ride,
a hell of a journey of painful insect bites
in an over-packed tourist boat,
almost over-turning in the foaming rough waters,
that speak volumes of commercial greed,
recalling the dangerous days of slavery!

Gorée!
Who owns Gorée?
Who will own up to Gorée?
A symbol of Africa's enslavement!
T'is easy for them to forget
the shame of Gorée!

Tiny Gorée!
Sixteen hectares of arid land,
where black hands broke hard rock,
where the blood of Africa
flowed like a red fountain,
to build out of stone and barren land,
where from Africa's coastlines,
angered oceans swelled and foamed,

as white pirates ships sailed away.

ENSLAVED AFRICA!
A HUMAN PRIZE OF GREED,
HATRED AND WAR!

Gorée!
This naked anus of white hatred!
A symbol of Africa's enslavement!
Who owns Gorée?
Who will own up to Gorée?
How easy t'is for them to forget
the shame of Gorée!

On the hilltops of Gorée,
between hungry Mouride young men
and wandering bare-breasted
white tourist women,
I saw rusted huge cannons
standing menacingly,
as in the old days of slavery,
when those bloody white "masters",
white "masters" after white "masters"
blasted, burned, maimed, raped,
renamed, and owned Africa!

Gorée!
This tiny gateway to hell!
Between Black Africa
and a Black Diaspora,
whose heritage?
whose anger?
whose shame?
who will own up to Gorée?
A symbol of Africa's enslavement!

In the blood-red "House of Slaves",
a tiny gate opens
into an endless blue ocean.

Ifi Amadiume   63

They call it "the gateway to hell",
between the devil and the deep blue sea,
lies a journey of no return!

Gorée!
This naked anus of white hatred!
A symbol of Africa's enslavement!
Who owns Gorée?
Who will own up to Gorée?
How easy t'is for them to forget
the shame of Gorée!

Oh! the choking in my throat!
Oh! the burning fire in my belly!
Oh how I burn
a fever nothing can quench,
safe the satisfaction of
naming, voicing, cursing:
Portugal, England, Dutchland, Frenchman!
Your "Good Road" was OUR HELL!!

(Dakar, Senegal, February 1992)

My Rasta Afrikan Brother

Between Camden Town,
all the way down
past Holloway Road,
on to Finsbury Park,
we have always met
and said "hello!"

Your face barely visible
beneath heavy locked Rasta hair!
In eyes that shine like yellow stars,
I always saw
something stronger than spoken words!

Rasta Afrikan brother,
wise child of my mother,
you ought to know,
deep down in my soul,
you will always be loved!

New World Order

"What is your name?"

"My game? Did you say?"

"Your name, I said!"

"Saddam Hussein"

"Sa-ddaam?"

"Saddam, the challenger!"

"Mine is George Bush!
President of America!
First man no mistake!
I make and unmake!"

"You make and unmake America?"

"Yeah! I am the world's only superpower!
I police the world!
I say who can do what!
I rule the world!" said George.

"What world?" asked Saddam.

"The world that includes Baghdad!" said George.

"Baghdad?
That cannot be
for I rule Baghdad!" exclaimed Saddam.

"No! I rule the world,
Kuwait and Baghdad!" roared George.

"No! I rule Baghdad and Kuwait!" shouted Saddam.

"One more word and we'll fight!" said George.

"Fight?
If we fight, I will win", said Saddam.

"You will lose!"

"I will win!"

"You will lose!"

"I will win!"

"Lose!"

"win!"

"Lose!"

"Win!"

"Look what I got", bragged George.

"What?" asked Saddam.

"See? Smart bombs in my left hand!
Nuclear ones in my right hand!
bullets packed pockets!
You see!" bragged George.

"Look what I've got!" yelled Saddam.

"What?" asked George.

"Arabs!" replied Saddam.

"I'll kick your ass!" shouted George

"Stop it, you two!" shouted a shocked little girl, playing nearby!
swift as a flash, she ran home to tell her mama of two small boys
planning to blow up the world!
"Mama, mama", she cried,
"Gosh mum!

Ifi Amadiume   67

"Oh my gosh!
"George is going for Saddam's arse, and . . . !"

"Good heavens! He did speak of kicking ass!" exclaimed mum.

(London, March 8, 1990)

There Will Be No Lies in Sarajevo

"Bosko Brckic and Admira Ismic, both 25, were shot dead on Wednesday trying to flee the besieged Bosnian capital to Serbia. Sweethearts since high school, he was a Serb and she a Muslim. . . They were shot at the same time, but he fell instantly and she was still alive. . . She crawled over and hugged him and they died like that, in each other's arms." THE GUARDIAN, May 24, 1993.

Death embrace on Vrbana Bridge,
Besieged Sarajevo's Miljacka River,
a wasteland of shell-blasted rubble,
downed tree branches,
dangling power lines;
the most dangerous place on earth,
it was said!

Talk processes,
no plans!
Savage war, Serbian guns.
More ethnic cleansing of Muslims!
More futile negotiations,
no plans!

X more people were killed.
More than X more injured.
More ethnic cleansing of Muslims!
Now by Serbs,
now by Croats!

Not if I could weep,
but I have wept!

In black draped voice,
deeper as the night grows,
I have filled funnels
with funeral oils
at the end of each day,

crying streams of tears,
as Sarajevo swims in hatred.

Today's verses are for the pure,
those who love,
in spite,
Admira Ismic,
Bosko Brckic,
butterflies of my verse,
sweethearts even in death!

You are no Romeo.
You are no Juliet.
There will be no lies
for savage murderers!
You died of bullet shots,
not of sweet daggers,
not of poisoned potions,
that death comforter
of tormented love.

You are no Romeo.
You are no Juliet.
You have died for
no worthy cause.
Admira and her Bosko,
shot in cold blood!
There will be no lies
for savage killers!

As their wasted, rotted flesh
fertilizes the wounded earth beneath,
Ismic says, "Love took them to their death.
That's proof this is not a war between Serbs
and Muslims. It's a war between crazy people,
between monsters. That's why their bodies
are still out there".

Ismic, wipe your tears man, I say,
the dead have buried themselves!

Rwanda

Ifi, what are
your feelings about
happenings in Rwanda?
What, my dear?

Rwanda? Blood!
Bloated bodies!
Butchered babies!
Fields of death!
Churches of death!
Streets of death!
Towns of death!
Villages of death!
Just death, death!
Just stench of death!

There are no tears
left to cry, my dear,
only this gaping,
huge hole inside
where it is a throbbing
in incessant pain
worse than death!

The blue Lake Victoria
is swollen,
filled with death!
Death, death, death!

There are no corners
left in my house
to run to and hide,
when the horrible
pictures are flashed,
for every nook and
corner has tasted

torrents of tears.
This is the picture
that won't go away.

Is it the small boy
picking droppings of grains
from charity sacks?

Is it the little child,
like Moses in a basket,
left for dead there
under the bushes,
but for the flickering
of an eye?

Oh, that I could not
rush her into my bosom!

Is it fields of kids
barbwired as their
sorrowful faces bear
testimony to a new
brutality of indifference,
at the end of history?
America's New World Order?

This is my answer
on Rwanda, Remember,
there are no corners
left to run to and hide.
Rwanda is the picture
that won't go away!

(Hanover, June 1994)

Ifi Amadiume

Behind the Burka

If I were an Afghan woman,
what would you an American
want to say to me?

I am an Afghan woman,
you are an American woman,
what have you said to me,
besides, take off your *burka*,
I give you books to read,
grains and cooking oil for meal,
medicine for your kids.

You forget to say,
I give you death,
I visit for days
with bomber planes!
I light up your night skies
with bombs, rockets, missiles!
I give you bullets,
gunshots for music!

Now you know,
a ghost took off the *burka*,
wanllai, not me!

I am waiting still behind the *burka*.

(Hanover, 1/1/03)

No Roads

If you want to see bad government,
go to Isolo.

If you know what okro is like,
how when you crush it,
when you mix it with water,
when you make okro soup,
that is the road in Isolo!
So if you want to see bad government,
go to Isolo.

Isolo where sandy roads slide slimily,
like okro soup cooked with mud.
Isolo where car tires slide from side to side,
screeching through muddy pits.
Isolo where smelling car rubbers,
stinking rubbish filled gutters join hands,
and poisonous fumes choke up air pipes,
as motorists and riders
knocked here and there fume in anger,
as blood pressures rise and fall again and again!
So if you want o see bad government,
go to Isolo.

Isolo where people look on knowingly,
hands raised to the sky,
because as they say,
what have we the people not done
to better our lives?
government simply greets us with lies!

Isolo where mama Bisi,
that grand old matriarch sees it all,
sitting by the road side,
selling real okro soup, egusi,
fried plantain, akara and moi moi.

So if you want to see bad government,
go to Isolo.

No Water

If you want to see bad government,
go to Abakpa.

If you know what a tap is like,
how when you half turn the knob,
water should gush out,
clear if it is clean,
sandy brown if it is dirty,
not so in Abakpa where the tap is dry,
not so in Abakpa where pipes are rusty red!

If you want to see bad government,
go to Abakpa.

Abakpa where Mama Ngozi says,
taps are not for water,
nobody in Abakpa turns on the tap!
only strangers from America touch a pump
and look for water!

If you want to see bad government,
go to Abakpa.

No Electricity

If you want to see bad government,
go to Nnobi.

If you know what a switch is like,
how when you press the button,
light breaks the darkness,
sometimes in brilliant flood of dazzling beams,
in Nnobi government light does not work!

If you want to see bad government,
go to Nnobi.

To think that in our beloved Motherland,
light problem reaches everywhere,
idle switches and sockets decorate white walls
in well off homes.
frustration, frustration is everywhere,
mixed with anger as they talk and talk!
poor governance, bad government!
poor development, bad democratization!

Isolo people talk of aid money,
millions of dollars from this place and that place!
In Abakpa they too know of aid money,
millions of dollars from this place and that place!
In Nnobi they ask what happens to all this money?
Why is it we have no roads, no water, no power?

If you want to see bad government,
go see daily lives
in Isolo,
in Abakpa,
in Nnobi,
in everywhere!

(August 9, 2002)

The Free Skyline

Out of their mighty head,
they block out all beauty!

They say, "See my ugly giant self".
And I say, "Get away from the free skyline"!

When jostling competitors build mighty towers,
they block off the distant hill lines,
along the free horizon.

When jostling competitors build shapeless squares
in grey concrete cement
and glazed glasses,
they hide the shading palms,
green grass and naked fields,
often even the blue of the sky,
the seasonal grays of the endless hills.

These jostling competitors block the free skyline,
the natural crown to pretty our pictures,
to cover the artist's hungry canvas.

We don't need more over-reaching towers
dwarfing our senses,
aren't we small enough
beneath a beautiful natural horizon!

Not Knowing Why!

No dilly dallying these days,
walking about W 116 street
in silence,
minding my business, alone.

Now I am always
peeping here and there,
saying a hello or hi,
even alaikum salaam,
in response to a stranger's
assalamu alaikum!
a well dressed lady from Mali,
a Senegalese man in a colorful gown,
perhaps someone from Dar-es-Salaam,
most likely a Mouride novice
from Mauritania,
even from Touba
with the white and black brick house,
for sure, always, a Tijaniyya
from Youssou N'dour's Dakar
sitting at the corner of Frederick Douglas
by the Lotto store,
in salaam flashes even white teeth!
a black woman with gold clips in her hair,
as if for luck she mimics to say salaam also,
several times,
gets a familiar smile from me,
not knowing why!

A Desolate Mother

Poetry comes to me
like a nice topping
on an extraordinary
feast-full night,
supped on
recollections of Bob Dylan's songs;
reflections on those joyous days
of unlimited expressions of freedom
though mixed with painful realities,
there still was no holding us back.

Where have all the hard-won freedoms gone?
What do we have but more realizations of pain,
stuck in sinking situations we cannot control.
Had we not struggled to minimize regression?
Didn't we think then it was all worth it?

By hard-won rights
I do not mean
lovers in pain,
the sort of pain
Dylan gave Sara,
then mournfully
sings to her
seductive songs,
saying, "forgive",
groaning his unworthiness!

What is the solace for me,
remembering those amazing times?
What is the comfort for me
reliving memories of lives well lived
in small,
sometimes
bigger than
small acts of defiance

Ifi Amadiume

to move things forward.

In my present pain,
I seek comfort,
perhaps more than that,
in the poet's vision of movements,
beyond stillness,
beyond apathy,
nearness beyond distance,
closeness in comradery,
compelling sounds
beyond the noise,
passing the desolation
locked inside.

In my present pain,
tell me,
which of
these fine mind-shifting words
can dissolve her sorrow;
the heavy
grief of a wounded mother,
sobbing by
the grave of a beloved daughter,
too young to die,
any child
too young to die.

(West Lebanon, October 2, 2005)

Animal Comrades

Mr/Madam Squirrel is daring out,
busily darting about,
jumping up and down
here and there.

Madam's mouth
is forever on the ground,
eating hungrily
from little droppings
on solid snow,
laid out
like white woolen carpet,
measured from wall to wall,
or should I say,
from trees to outside wall.

Madam Cat too dared out,
doing her own quaint thing,
coming out just once
the other day,
walking daintily
on a snow white backyard,
so evident
not to her taste at all!

You could say
Jack Frost had the upper hand,
but for the daring birds out there,
black crows eating through thick and thin,
weathering this unpredictable temperament
of a confused winter in March,
or should I say
global warmings and changing times.

(West Lebanon, March 16, 2007)

My Animal Ozone Environ Mental Life

There is always a first,
not always as clear
as day and night,
as I say
to my local gray
and red squirrel friends.
Do you know what?
There is a bigger world out there.
So, away from snow white,
on a nice visit
and a nice day,
I saw a jet black squirrel,
wagging a bushy tail,
smiling at me
in should I say,
a Syracuse serenade!
Let's say that's
a first time
in my animal
ozone environ
mental life!

(West Lebanon, April 11, 2007)

Only One Comrade

Mate squirrel,
busy like me,
in all weather,
loosens the grounds,
plants the bulbs
molded by her.
She is now the rain-sounder
with Madam Cat's absence
from conference,
intimidated or disgusted
I don't know which!
That's the struggle
Madam Cat has to deal with,
missing in action,
cause she is sorting out
this situation
of an Oduche,
in this day and age,
locking up a big woman in a box,
letting her out
to answer nature's calls
how and when he pleases!

He tells me to
come see my snake.
In a Royal Python lying there immobilized,
I see a big woman disarmed,
I see many women deactivated,
just like Madam Cat!
No crows marching!
No birds pecking!
No cats watching!
Only one Comrade out there!

(West Lebanon, April 29, 2007)

Like the Deleb-Palm

(Hausa saying: "Inuwar giginya, na nesa kan sha sanyinki."
Translation: "Shade of the Deleb palm-tree, those furthest
away enjoy your shade.")

Write freely,
think freely,
do not hide in borrowed words
and borrowed styles,
searching for rhymes;
your language is rhythm,
your anger rhythmic,
say what you see.

Let the world see the mess,
the emptiness of their minds,
the bankruptcy of their brains.
Search and search for their hearts.

The rains no longer come
in their seasons,
the heavens send hot piss on us,
the plants wither and die,
the wounded lands show their gashes,
the forests are burnt to ashes,
the animals starve and die.

Did you all not feel the disease?
sometimes the reason why?
They bought the mouths of the diviners,
they made them not to find it!
The old sons of the soil still found it!
They found it and said it,
said it like the sons of the land,
in the ways of our great ancestors,
who like grazing cattle
were chased away from their pastures,
they were left to feed on sand!

Over the distance across the river,
our ancestors watched, they saw
the multitude landing,
suddenly new things that shone,
beautiful things that shimmer in the sun
appeared over there,
there on a land they once knew,
over the distance across the river,
a different herd of cattle was feeding fat,
eating freely from fresh pastures of the land!

The old sons of the soil saw all this,
with tears in their hearts,
mist in their eyes,
they saw the thieving!

The old sons of the soil always knew,
they always knew of the denial,
they always knew of the betrayal
they saw the fast diminishing greens!

The old sons of the soil
knew of the things under the soil,
the liquids that flowed,
the stones that shone.

Now with tears in their eyes,
hot tears of the betrayed,
the humiliated,
they watched their shade,
the tree they planted and fed,
now this tree they had tended,
like the Deleb-palm,
useless in itself,
bends over its head
to shade another,
a shade denied to
its own feeders for so long!

Ifi Amadiume

I stood and watched,
I looked at the old sons of the soil,
I looked at the leanness,
I looked at the hungry children,
the idle youth, so full of life,
they were like abandoned cattle
stranded on a sandy shore
across the distance,
looking on green pastures
no longer their own.

Then I knew we were waiting.
Then I knew the bad tree will be uprooted,
right from the roots;
a different tree will be planted.